cool jazz

Arranged by James Sodke and Brent Edstrom

contents

ISBN 978-0-634-02555-6

HAL•LEONARD®

7777 W. BLUEMOUND RD. P.O. BOX 13819 MILWAUKEE, WI 53213

Visit Hal Leonard Online at
www.halleonard.com

ALL BLUES

By MILES DAVIS

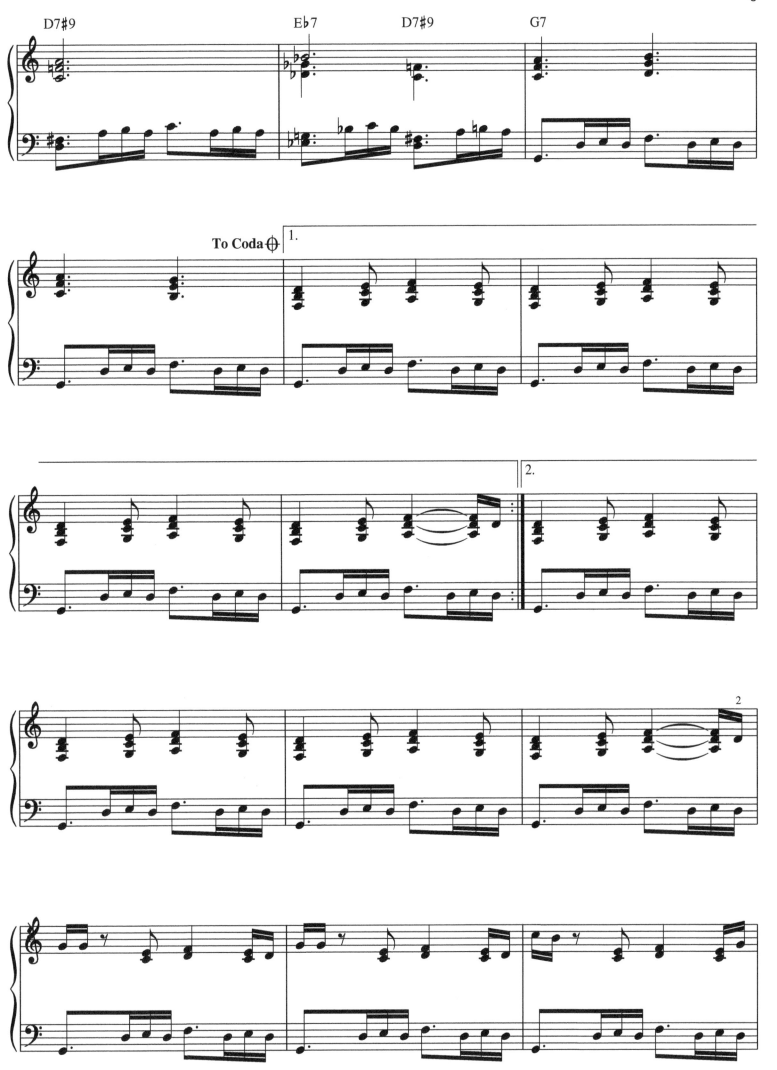

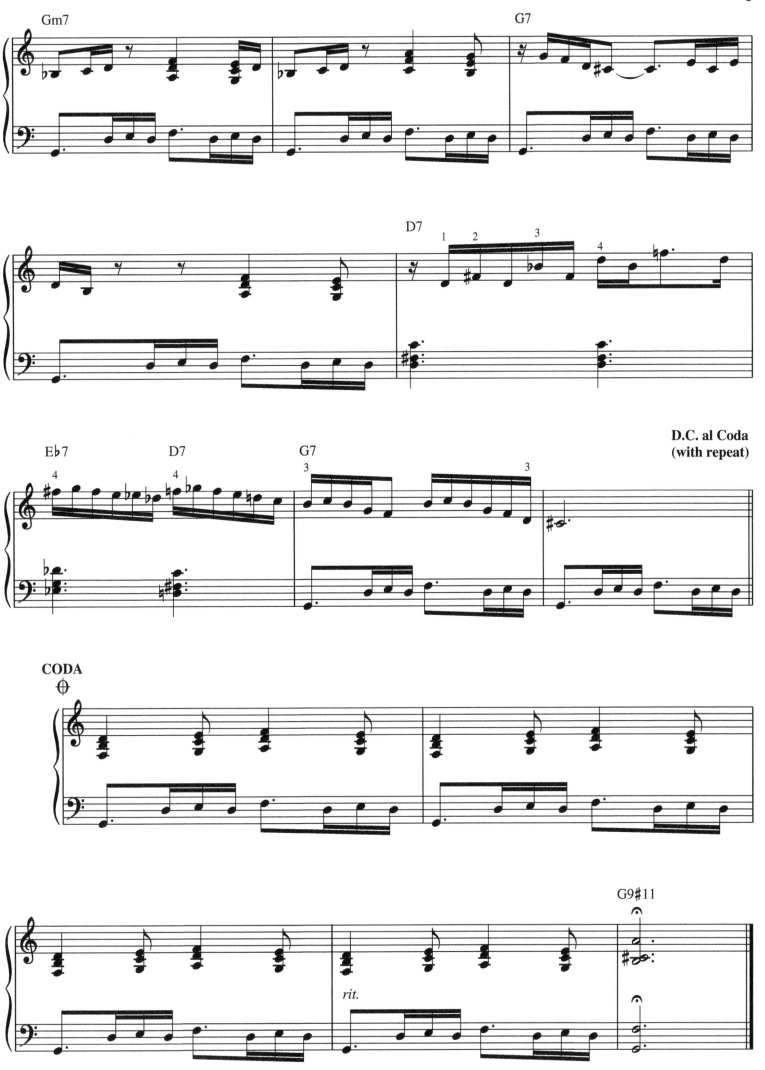

BACKGROUND MUSIC

By WAYNE MARSH

A BALLAD

By GERRY MULLIGAN

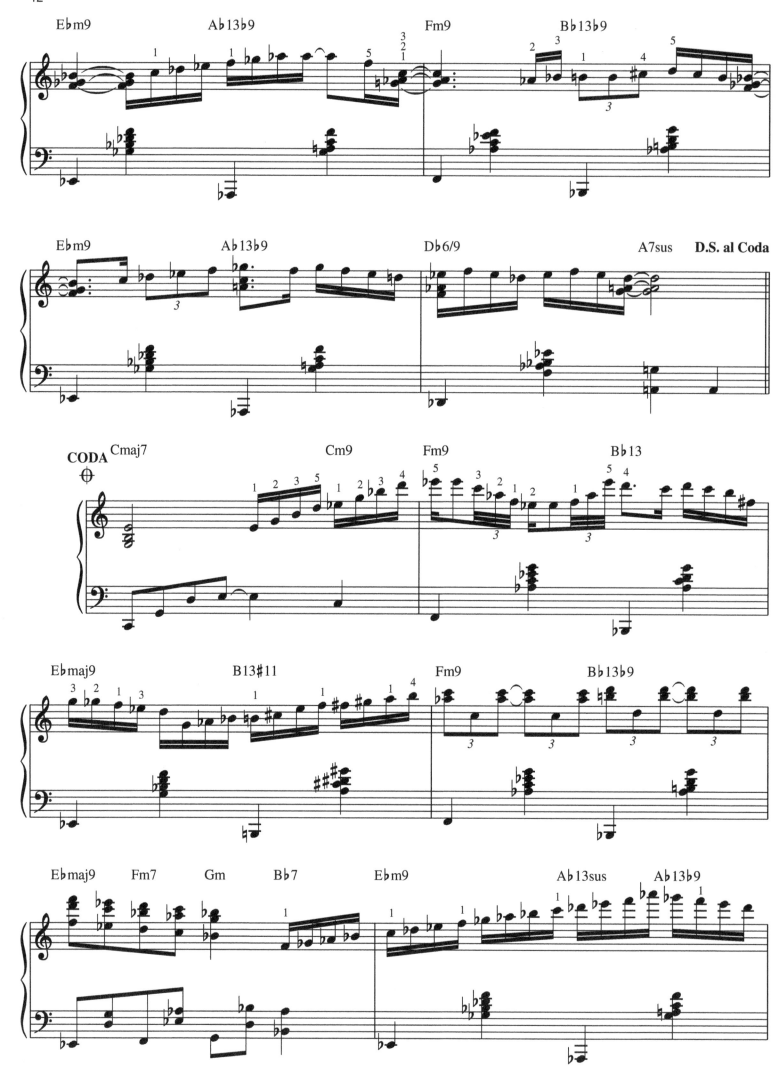

BLUE IN GREEN

By MILES DAVIS

CAST YOUR FATE TO THE WIND

Music by VINCE GUARALDI

Moderately, with a beat

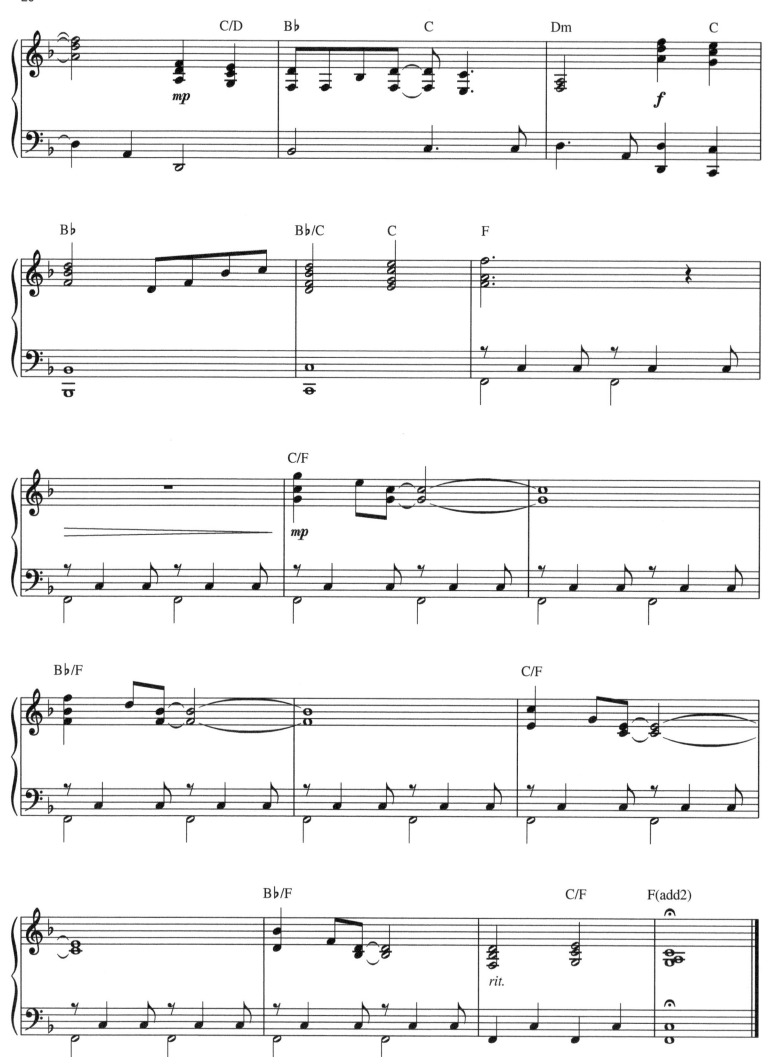

CON ALMA

By JOHN "DIZZY" GILLESPIE

CONCEPTION

By GEORGE SHEARING

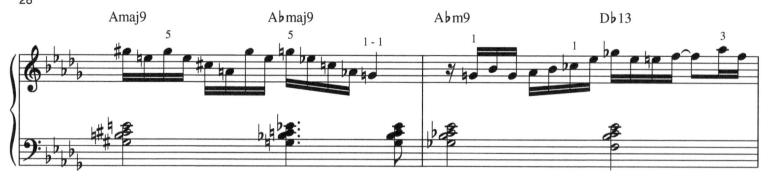

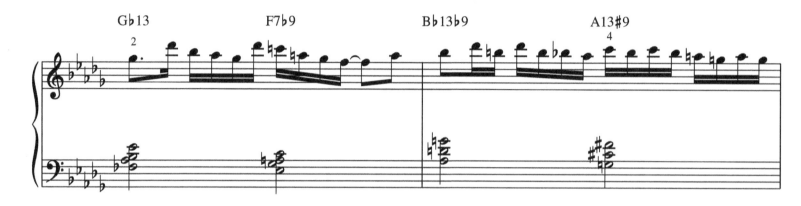

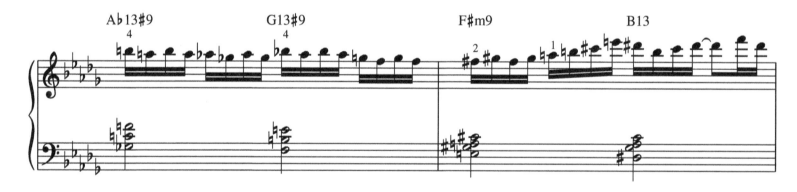

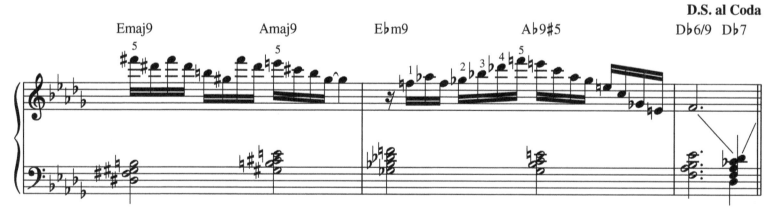

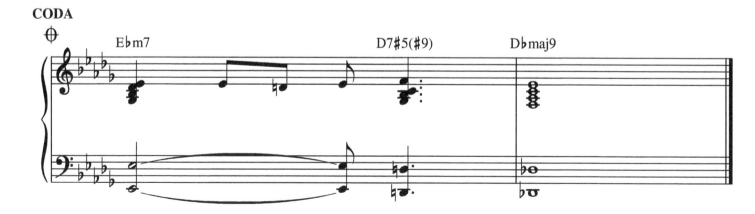

ERNIE'S BLUES

By ERNIE WILKINS

CROSSCURRENT

By LENNIE TRISTANO

34

DJANGO

By JOHN LEWIS

EPISTROPHY

By THELONIOUS MONK
and KENNY CLARKE

Medium Swing

FIVE BROTHERS

By GERRY MULLIGAN

ISRAEL

By JOHN CARISI

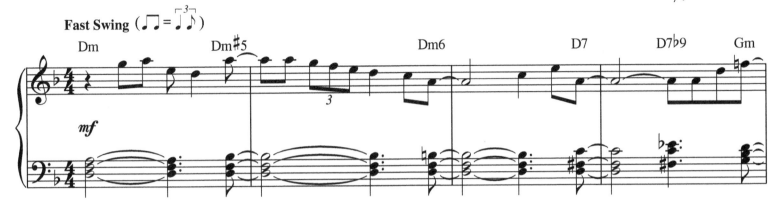

50

JAMBANGLE

Written by GIL EVANS

KILLER JOE

By BENNY GOLSON

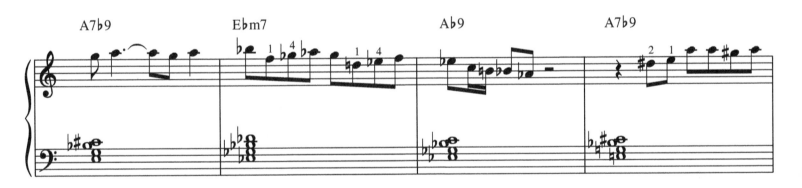

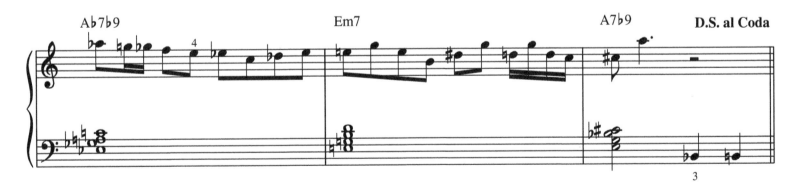

JERU

By GERRY MULLIGAN

LULLABY OF BIRDLAND

Words by GEORGE DAVID WEISS
Music by GEORGE SHEARING

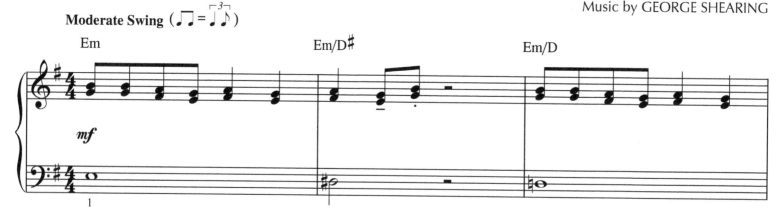

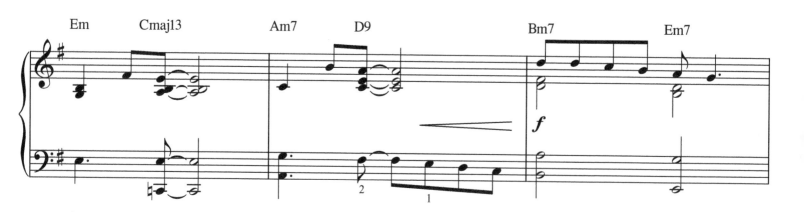

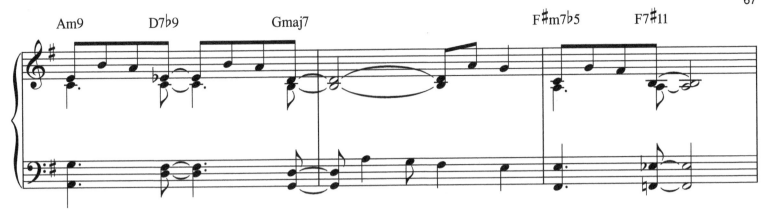

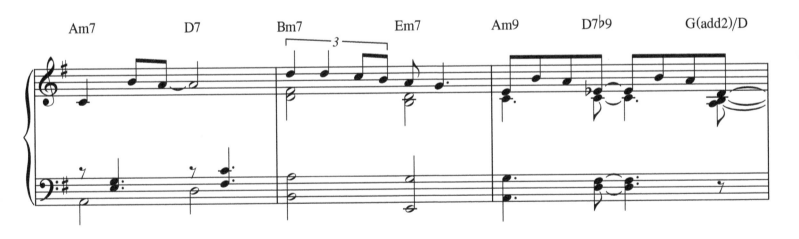

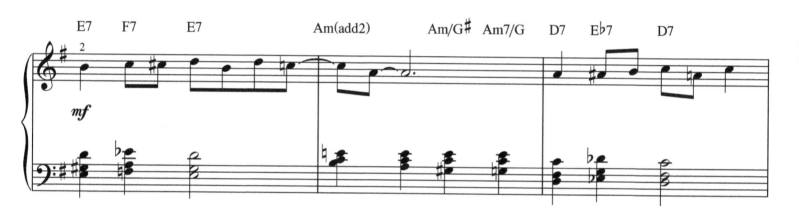

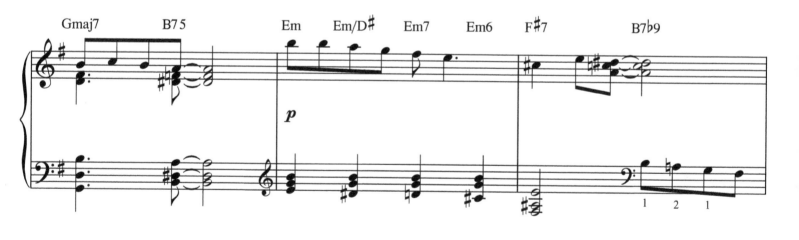

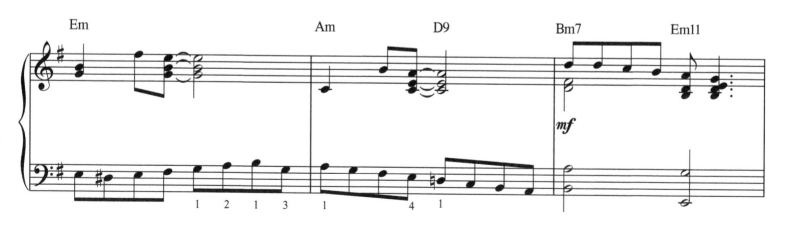

NARDIS

By MILES DAVIS

To Coda

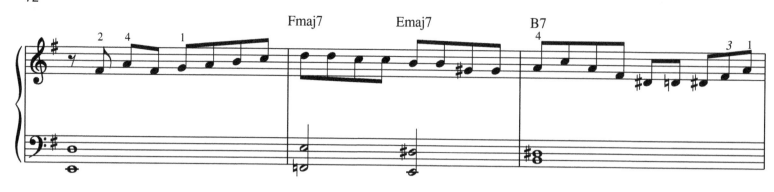

OFF MINOR

By THELONIOUS MONK

To Coda

SO WHAT

By MILES DAVIS

STELLA BY STARLIGHT

Words by NED WASHINGTON
Music by VICTOR YOUNG

TAKE FIVE

By PAUL DESMOND

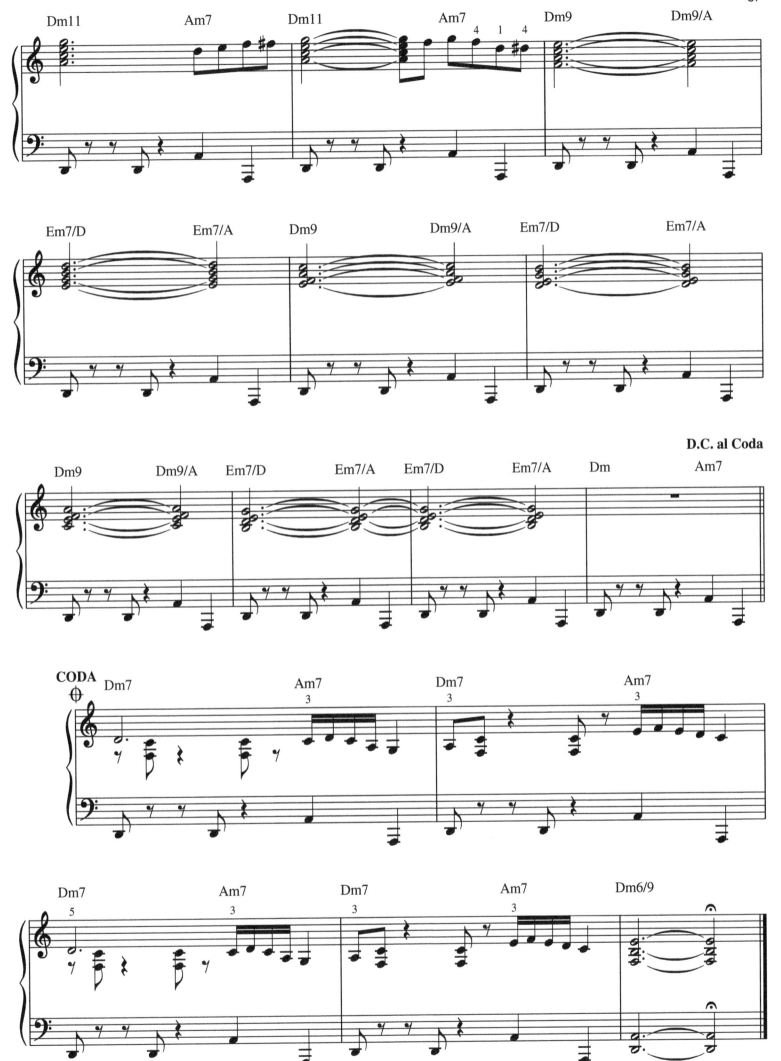

WHISPER NOT

By BENNY GOLSON

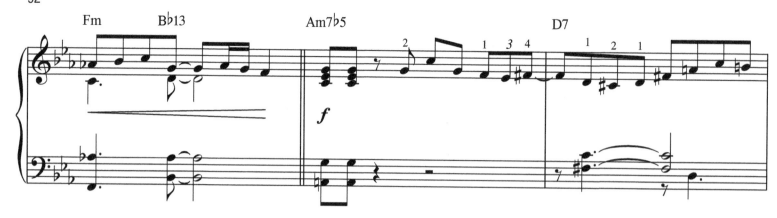

WALTZ FOR DEBBY

Lyric by GENE LEES
Music by BILL EVANS